TEEN LIFE

Everything a Teenager Should Know
to Survive the Teen Years

BY

D. M. MEJIAS

To my mother,

from whom I learned resilience,

and to JJ

for your love and support.

We are what we repeatedly do; excellence, then, is not an act but a habit.

~ Aristotle

Stuff in This Book

STUFF IN THIS BOOK

Stuff in This Book

STUFF IN THIS BOOK

Making Friends and Fitting In

"It takes a long time to grow an old friend."
~ John Leonard

You are either the new kid or just want to expand your circle of friends. Well, alright! Congratulations! There are literally hundreds of potential new friends at your school and most likely they are also looking to expand their circle of friends.

First thing you have to do is relax; people like to hang around cool, calm, and collected people. Teens have a lot of stresses in their lives, as you already know, and the friends they choose are people who are relaxed, fun and real. They want to relax and unwind from the pressures of their teen lives. So relax and be cool. Don't appear too anxious. People will sense this and won't want to hang with you.

Where do we look for friends? Well, you need to find out where you fit in. Let's find your group. Think of an activity or hobby you enjoy. The following are some activity ideas:

comic books	dance	video games

Teen Life

music band	chess	cheerleading
sports	volunteering	poetry
collecting	acting	water sports

Once you decide on an activity you enjoy join a club at school, online or in your community. If there are no clubs around your area or school, you can always talk to an adult or school teacher to help you start one. There you will meet people who share the same passion and excitement for your hobby that you do. In fact, sharing common interests is a great kick-starter to form a friendship. Find someone who shares your same interests and you'll create an instant bond. Once you meet those people, get to know them. Find out more about them. You never know, you might have more than one interest in common.

Another way to meet new people is on a social network such as Twitter. On some of these social networks you can meet people from all over the world. Browse profiles by your interests and you will find people who enjoy the same things you do. When they post interesting comments reply to them with a friendly post. Post interesting things about the things you like and people who share your interests will share those posts and sometimes reply to you. I have made a few friends this way. Do not beg anyone to follow you and don't be a stalker, that actually scares people away.

Let them follow you if they find you interesting. Always use caution while on the internet because people may not be who they say they are. Make sure you read the chapter titled, "Internet Safety."

With the permission of your parents, of course, you can throw a party! Get some party food and drinks. Get the latest sounds or ask your parent to hire a DJ. Invite lots of people from your school and you have a party! People like to go to a party where everybody who's anybody is there. So make sure you invite all the cool people you want to get to know. Everybody loves a good

3

party and this is a great way to meet friends. At a party, people just want to have fun and are more open to talk to you. Strike a conversation and see where it goes. Remember don't force it. Let it flow and never fake who you are or the things and activities you like. We are trying to meet people who share your interests and your personality. Fake friendships don't last. So, again, keep it real.

Dress cool. If you are a boy, browse the latest style magazines for men like *GQ* or *Vogue* for men. If you are a girl, check out the fashion magazines such as *InStyle*. Or pay attention to the cool styles in your town or school. Then go to your closet and see if you can come up with a cool outfit. If you have some funds, you can always hit the mall and get a happening outfit.

Get your hair done. Again, pay attention to what's in style at your school or check out some teen magazines like *Seventeen, Teen Vogue, J-14,* or *M* magazine for the latest hairstyles, and enter your party like you own the place. Well, you do!

If you are a girl that wants to befriend another girl, you can complement her outfit or hair. Just approach her and then say how much you like her shoes or clothes and that it seems you have similar taste in clothes. Then you can say something like "we definitely have to go shopping together."

Another way to make a friend is if you see someone that needs help, offer your assistance. If someone drops their books, help them pick them up. If you hear someone needing something and you know you can help, then offer to help. This is an easy way to make a new friend.

Now that you have some friends, you have to know how to keep them. Listen to your friends. Don't monopolize the conversation let them share their thoughts so that you both can talk about them. Ask them how their day is going and genuinely care about their well-being. Let them make decisions about where you guys are going or what you are going to do today. Keep conversations light and upbeat don't talk about negative issues and if you do, end it on a good note.

Be trustworthy, never lie or betray your friend or you will lose them forever. Be there for your friend, if you can, when they need you. Be loyal to your friend. Remember their birthday. Be there if your friend needs support, a shoulder to cry on or just someone to listen. If you follow these guidelines you will increase your chances of having a friend for life!

Being Popular

"Avoid popularity if you would have peace."

~ Abraham Lincoln

What makes someone popular? Is it their clothes, their hair, their personality? Well, it is a combination of all these things to different degrees. Popular people sometimes look different; have their own styles and personalities. But most of them have one thing in common. Charisma. "What is charisma?" you ask. Charisma is defined as a personal quality that gives a person influence over other people. They have a certain magnetism that attracts people. They are confident and they know what to say at the right time. In other words, they have people skills. People skills is the ability to deal, influence and communicate well with all kinds of people.

To be popular you need to put yourself out there. Don't be shy. You have nothing to lose and popularity to gain. So let's go. Be confident, make small talk and see how it goes.

At first, you may feel uncomfortable and that's alright. You are probably not used to getting out of your comfort zone. Be yourself and being yourself right now means you want to meet lots of people like you and make lots of friends. It takes practice.

People like many different qualities in other people. They may like how they feel when they hang with you. They may like the way you dress or how smart you are. They may like you because you are good at sports, are pretty or have a great sense of humor. The possibilities are endless. So let's address the things that make someone likable and popular.

Charisma: Charismatic people are charmers. They say things people want to hear. They make people feel good about themselves. They are polite. They are upbeat and fun. They are confident, comfortable and happy about who they are and it shows. They are genuinely and tastefully funny. They are relaxed. They can relate to what others are feeling and be supportive and helpful. They treat people as they want to be treated. They actively listen when someone speaks. They make people feel important by remembering people's names, birthdays or things they said in the past. They compliment people and easily receive compliments. Some people are not natural charmers, but by working on it they can become the most charming person around.

Clothes: OK so not everybody can afford designer clothes, but you can still look like a winner. You can get a fashion magazine and look at what's in style or just pay attention to what's in style at your school. Then get similar outfits at stores like American Eagle, Aeropostale, Hollister, Urban Outfitters, Old Navy, Gap, Buckle and Abercrombie & Fitch. Wal-Mart and Target have some cool clothes, check them out. Your local second-hand stores often have treasures. You can also go to Polyvore.com and ask for assistance from other users or just browse their favorite outfits! Now that you are already attracting all this attention with your new duds, let's talk about that "do."

Hair: OMG, if you are one of those people that has been getting haircuts from grandma please, stop. It's time to grow up. There are many inexpensive places that can give you a stylish look. Find a magazine or a picture of the latest hair styles and show it to your hairdresser. She will help you select the best style for your type of face. Alright, now you are really looking hot…people have been noticing the new you. There you go. Let's work on other stuff now.

Lifestyle: People generally enjoy people who are interesting. If you are not already doing great and interesting things then you

8

need to get into something. Think of something you enjoy and always wanted to do but never got around to doing it. Join a club of your hobbies. Try out for a sport like football, wrestling, track, baseball or tennis. Learn to play a musical instrument like the guitar, piano, strings or drums. Learn how to surf or scuba dive.

Volunteer with the elderly, at a children's hospital or the local homeless shelter. Volunteering is an admirable way to get instant wisdom on life. You will grow as a person and you will be helping others! You can also check out the Peace Corps, study abroad, or open your own business. That's right, just because you are a teen does not mean you cannot have your own business. Think of something that is needed but not available for sale. Create a website that offers something people may want or need. Write a blog. Write a book. Talk to your parents or check out the Small Business Administration website for teens or *Entrepreneur* magazine's site for young people. These sites have great resources and ideas on businesses you can open right now. There are endless hobbies and interests out there, so get out and look and you'll be surprised by the riches you'll find.

Love: Getting Ready for Love

"Love is but the discovery of ourselves in others, and the delight in the recognition."

~ Alexander Smith

There are some things we need to address before dating. You need to be ready to enter one of the most challenging, and at the same time beautiful, stages in your life, but proceed with caution. Do it when you are ready and not because you are lonely. Listen to your parent's advice. They DO know better. Now follow these steps to get ready:

1. Know Yourself: The first thing you need to do before you start dating is know yourself. Know the core of you or what is important to you (e.g. your morals and values). There are many questions you should ask yourself. The following are a few important ones that can easily make or break a relationship:

What do I want out of life?

What are my goals and dreams?

What is important to me in a mate?

How do I want to be treated?

Do I want children? ♥

If my mate has different religious beliefs, would that matter to me?

Typically, the best partner for you would be someone who answers in a similar fashion. If you had a hard time answering these questions it means you still don't know yourself well and dating should be approached with caution because you may change while you are dating and after that you and your love may not be compatible anymore. Your views change as you get older. The things that you liked as a teenager, for example, may not be the same things you like as an adult. The people you accept into your life when you are a teenager may not be the same people you accept later in life. Believe me, you will change. Therefore, if you get involved in a relationship when you are younger as you get older you may not have the same things in common with your sweetheart anymore. Even adults go through this change. As we grow older we evolve and sometimes grow apart. It is best to have a good idea of who you are and let your true self be known to your sweetheart. ♥

It is possible to date someone with different opinions and likes, but be aware that this can only be achieved by two very understanding, patient and flexible people. There will be differences of opinions and this sometimes damages a relationship if not handled properly. Some couples are able to get through these differences fine, but it is very challenging. Those people, I've noticed, are very intelligent, evolved and wise. In my life, I've met many couples and I have noticed that it makes for a long, successful relationship when both of you share the same values, similar likes and life philosophies.

2. Know the kind of person you want: Know what personality traits and values you're looking for in a sweetheart and stick to them. Don't focus your dating on looks alone. For a successful and lasting relationship, you have to look for a combination of looks, personality and values. Looks alone don't work in the long run.

3. How to find the kind of person you want: You would have to look in the places those people frequent. For example, if you are looking for an ambitious person that is self-sufficient, go to business seminars. If you are looking for a studious type of person go to your local library. In other words, frequent the places where the kind of people you want to meet hang out.

4. Don't lie or misrepresent yourself: By all means, don't lie or pretend to be someone you are not. It will come to the surface eventually and your loved one will NOT trust you after that. Thus, do not make someone fall in love with you under false pretenses. You will hurt, disillusion and damage them and they may lose trust in everybody not just you. You don't want that on your shoulders. Once you are in a relationship, they will get to know you and see the real you! They will resent you and the relationship will NOT work because you are not who you said you were or what they were looking for to begin with! So be truthful and you will attract people who like the real you.

5. Take pride in you: Please take care of your appearance. Take pride in how you look. Get a hairstyle that suits your face.

Love: Getting Ready for Love

Exercise and be healthy. Floss your teeth. If you just brush, food substances that are caught between your teeth just stay there rotting and your breath will smell like something died in there. So floss! For those guys out there that just grab the first wrinkled and dirty shirt they see on the floor to wear on a date, please don't. You should wash your clothes after you wear them once. Or else, you will smell. And please iron your clothes. Wrinkles have never been in unless you buy a shirt that's supposed to be wrinkled. That's the only exception; don't try to pass your wrinkled and stinky shirt for one that is supposed to be wrinkled. We know the difference. And by all means, use deodorant! Believe me we can smell you when you don't. And finally, some fragrance will be nice. Oh, please use fragrance in conjunction with deodorant, not as a supplement for deodorant. Don't be the guy with the body odor masked in heavy cologne; yes, we have all endured him! Some popular perfume suggestions are: For boys – Drakkar, CK, Blue Jeans. Jean Paul Gaultier Le Male, Carolina Herrera are very popular. For girls, CK, CK2, Jean Paul Gaultier, Lovely by Sarah Jessica Parker, and Dolce & Gabbana Light Blue are also popular. If you lack funds, you can always go to your local pharmacy and purchase little samples of some of these fragrances.

6. Be happy: Be happy with yourself and your life. If you are not happy, then fix what's making you unhappy. Work on it and then date. You can still date someone while you are working on yourself, but be conscientious about it. When people date someone that is not at their best emotionally they might move on to someone that has it together and are more suitable for them. Be aware of your emotional state and do NOT take it out on your loved one. Know that person's wants and needs, theirs may be different from yours.

♥

7. Correct your issues: Try to correct your issues or baggage before getting into a relationship. If you are a jealous person or have trust issues because someone cheated on you in the past, try to correct these by reading self-help books or working with a professional. Not all people are cheaters. As a matter of fact, the National Science Foundation's General Social Survey, which has used a national representative sample to track the opinions and social behaviors of Americans since 1972, shows that in any given year about 10 percent of married people — 12 percent of men and 7 percent of women — say they have had sex outside of their marriage. That means that about 90 percent of people don't engage in extra marital affairs! If you have commitment issues try to find out why. Why are you afraid of commitment? There are many issues people deal with; you should try to correct yours before putting yourself out there. Always try to be the best version of you.

8. Be friends first: When you meet someone, take your time and get to know them first so that you can see who they <u>really</u> are in different situations. People are usually on their best behavior when you first meet. Don't think this is who they really are. Wait a while and see how that person is in different situations or else you may get a big surprise later. This happens with a lot of people. I have a few friends that got together quickly, even moved in together, and then BOOM. "I didn't know he was capable of that." Surprise! Your prince charming is actually a big fat frog. Pay close attention to see if his or her life plans — career goals, children and other future plans — fit yours. So control those hormones and take your time getting to know people and what they want out of life. If they are not a match, don't despair, it just means your sweetheart is still out there looking for you!

Love: How to Make Them Fall in Love

"Unable are the loved to die, for love is immortality"
~ Emily Dickinson

♥ In this section I will give you some advice on how to make them fall in love with you. This is the magic question in a lot of people's minds, especially young ones. After you have read the last section on dating tips then practice the following tips:

1. Once you see that person in a room, stand up straight and confident and look at them for a few seconds. Make sure they see you looking at them. Once you catch their attention, look away and look down at something you have in your hands or just your hands. This will let them know you may be interested and pick their curiosity. If you are in a group of people where someone is talking, pay more attention to your person of interest than the speaker. Keep gazing back to your person of interest. Again, make sure they know you are looking at them. Don't say a word yet. This has the possibility of creating excitement.

18

How to Make Them Fall in Love

2. Find out what you can about that person with your friends without sounding like a stalker and then see if you have anything in common with them. If they like to read and you do too, make sure they notice. If they like a certain band and you do too, again make sure they know. Find what you have in common and subtly show them. Don't go up to them out of nowhere and say, "Hey, I heard you like to read!" You will sound too desperate and creepy. In other words, make sure they notice you have a hobby or something in common. This is great for a conversation starter. Or carry an unusual object, their favorite book, or something they will notice and want to talk to you about. Please don't fake anything because eventually they will know you were faking and you would look like a desperate idiot.

3. Be polite always, not just in front of them. Be comfortable with yourself, talk to them like you would talk to an old buddy. Watch your language though. Be easy going, casual and respectful. If you bump into them, be polite, wait a split second then look at them and smile. Big smile. As if you are happy to see an old childhood friend.

4. Don't act too interested at the beginning. Keep the mystery alive. If you are going out with a group of friends invite the person. Not like a date yet! Don't rush and be too obvious. Act like you like them as a friend and want to hang out with them and your friends and get to know them.

5. Once you are friends, be a great listener. Repeat what they say to you often to let them know you understand. Don't interrupt them to offer advice. If they want to speak, let them. Only give advice if they ask. Listen... Look them in the eyes and don't fidget. Fidgeting makes you look like you are bored and can't wait to get out of there. If you listen well and frequently repeat what they say, they will think you are the easiest person to talk to and possibly start to fall for you.

6. Make sure to show them that you are husband or wife material. Everybody likes to bring home a great person. Become that great person. It's survival of the fittest out there and people like a great provider; a person that will defend and stand up for their family, friends or a stranger if need be; a polite human being and well-mannered person; an ambitious person who is going places in life and who has plans for the future, like a great career; a caring person that treats everybody with respect and kindness, especially their parents and the elderly. A great person is someone that is respectful to children and has manners when it comes to dealing with strangers. A person who treats everybody with respect and kindness without wanting anything in return will treat their spouse well. Be that person. If you go to a restaurant with them, remember to be polite and considerate with the staff.

This is not just this time people. You should always behave in this manner.

7. When you talk, pay attention to her body language; if she starts to fidget, she is bored! You probably have been going on and on. Change the subject. Don't push it! Or ask something about her and let her talk for a while.

8. If you don't know what to talk about ask questions about them and get to know them. Find out interesting and fun facts about your town or your family and talk about them. Don't brag. Never talk about your achievements or accomplishments out of the blue. Let him find out later, subtly, or if he asks. Nobody likes a show off.

9. Always match your mood to hers. Never act like you just won the lottery when she is frustrated with work or school. Always match your mood. Be empathetic always.

10. Be a problem solver. If they are in need, show them what a good person you are and offer to help. If you can surprise them with something they need or have been looking for even better.

How to Make Them Fall in Love

Don't fake it, be yourself.

Be patient, if things don't work out that just means you have not found your soul mate. He is out there. So start your exciting love adventure and find him. This is what has worked for me. It may not work for you. But you don't lose anything with trying. Good Luck! ☺

Love: How To Treat Your Loved One

"At the touch of love, everyone becomes a poet."

~ Plato

These are the best bits of advice I've gathered from my life experiences and friends; some of them are obvious, but some people out there might need a little help.

1. Make sure you compliment your significant other every day. This will make them feel good and they will associate feeling good with being with you. Compliment their mind, body and soul.

2. Don't nitpick. See the big picture. What is more important: for them to feel good with you or you winning this argument? Think about it. Think! Too many arguments will eat away at the romance and you will end up with a stale relationship. So let them win and don't argue!

3. Let them be themselves. If you don't like what you see or who they are, too late. You should have taken the time to get to know

24

them BEFORE getting involved in a relationship with them. Don't try to change them now! That's why it's better to take the time to get to know people before getting involved to see if they are a match. Don't get involved and then try to change them! That will just be a disaster, trust me.

4. Let them know once in a while how much you appreciate them. Pay attention, there is ALWAYS something to appreciate about them.

5. Do apologize immediately after you lose your temper or say something you shouldn't have. Don't let them fester!!! This reminds me of the next rule.

6. Don't go to bed angry. Apologize. You have to choose your battles. Is it more important to state your point or for your relationship to go down on the love scale?

7. Listen more than you talk. Do not interrupt and listen! Respond to what they are saying with not only words but eye contact. Eye contact is VERY important guys! Can't you tell when someone is just holding on to their seats waiting to get their

own views out? They can tell this about you too!

8. Spend quality time with each other and create new memories frequently to deepen your love and friendship.

9. Compromise if you want to do different things. Today we do your thing and tomorrow we do mine. Don't monopolize or she may leave for someone that actually cares about she wants to do!

♥

10. Don't argue. If there are differences of opinions try to talk it out. If there is no resolution, look at the big picture again. Consider how much you want this person in your life and let him "have" this one.

11. DO have your own interests and hobbies. Don't make him your whole life. It puts a big burden on his shoulders. That's a big responsibility and a burden! Have your own separate life; meaning hobbies and interests you enjoy doing.

12. Don't argue in front of other people. Keep your relationship and discussions private.

♥

13. Don't ever laugh at your sweetheart's expense. How do you

think this will make YOU feel if it was the other way around? Think about it. You are embarrassing her. If she ever makes a blunder in public, subtly change the subject or create a distraction to take the focus off of her. She will thank you later and know that you will always have her back. You knight in shining armor, you. Or princess....ahem, if you are a girl.

14. Do NOT correct your boo in public!! Again, don't embarrass him.

15. Support your sweetheart's goals and dreams. Let him be himself so that he can grow and evolve. This often means allowing him the freedom to "error" knowing that sometimes he will also succeed. Nobody likes to be told what to do. That's his parents' job!

♥

16. Communicate. Say what you want or what's bothering you. This is very important, especially in the beginning when you are getting to know each other. Your sweetheart cannot read your mind, but he can learn to understand how you communicate and how you love if you communicate and let him know. You may also want to read "The Five Love Languages" by Gary Chapman. This book elaborates on the different ways people show love and how they want to receive it.

17. Never do something that would put you in a position where you have to lie to your partner. Don't do it, period! If telling them the truth of what you did will hurt them, then **DON'T DO THE ACTION!** If you feel you want to do something that is going to hurt your sweetheart and you are going to have to lie to her, then you need to reassess your feelings for her.

18. Keep your promises. Show your partner your words have value.

19. When both of you agree to something, like a budget, stick to it! Don't change things later without discussing it with them. Come on…!

20. Don't treat your sweetheart as a possession. They are a human being with their own individual wants and needs that need to be met for happiness and growth.

♥

21. When you are married and both work, divide the house chores. It is not fair just because you happened to be of a certain…ehem… gender that you should do all the work. No!

22. When tempted to argue stop yourself. Talk it over and by all means do not bring in past hurts. That will not help your relationship move forward. Leave the past in the past and concentrate on the present.

23. As soon as temptation appears REMOVE yourself! DO NOT GO THERE! The grass is the same on all sides after a while. Believe me!

24. Make sure you remember birthdays, anniversaries and other special dates. Do whatever you have to do to remember. By doing this, you'll make your sweetie feel important and loved.

♥

25. Make a mental note about what they like when you two go shopping (This should be why guys go to the mall with their spouses or girlfriends). Remember what she made a fuss about and then surprise her for her birthday or anniversary with the item they love! She will love you for making her feel so treasured. Girls usually like to get flowers (get to know your sweetie just in case she's one of those girls who doesn't like flowers), jewelry, purses and latest styles. Teen girls love teddy bears, flowers, concert tickets, chocolates, candy, dinner, clothes, jewelry, perfumes, shoes or something she collects. Boys usually like concert tickets, clothes, shoes, cologne, electronics, gadgets, or whatever he collects.

26. If you are in a bad mood, tell your sweetheart that you are not feeling like yourself and need your own space for a while until you feel better. You don't want to be rude to your honey and they will appreciate the honesty. Follow these things and your sweetheart will be happy and very enamored with you.

Best Friends

"A friend is one who walks in when others walk out."

~ Walter Winchell

These are the people with whom you share yourself deeply, your emotions, wants, needs and secrets. With them you form the strongest kind of friendship, the kind that will last a lifetime. These are the people who are going to be with you through everything, good times and bad. The following are qualities that a good friend must possess:

Trustworthy: means you don't talk about what was said to you in confidence. You keep your friend's secrets to yourself. You don't gossip or talk about your friend in a way that can be construed as negative, ever! Be a person of your word. If you say something, mean it. Never go back on your word. Think before you are going to say something so that you don't regret it later.

Loyal: means you always take your friend's side in public, even if in private you disagree. One who takes a friend's side, even if at that time that side is the unpopular one, is a true friend.

Caring: means to truly want the best for your friend, not what is best for you. A good friend is someone that always has your best interests at heart. They will give you good advice. Sometimes that advice is not what you want to hear, but deep inside you know they are right and their advice is coming from a place of love.

Good listener: means you actually look your friend in the eye when they are talking to you and actually absorb what they are saying. Do not just brush off what they are saying and move on to another topic. You would not want someone to do that to you and make you feel that what you are saying is not important. It makes you friend feel just like that, "not important." So listen to your friend when they need you to listen and offer advice only when they ask.

Keeps in touch: Good friends keep in touch when they are apart. It shows them how much you really treasure the friendship. If your friend is out of town, call once in a while just to check in and find out how things are going for them. It makes them feel you truly care.

Best Friends

Sometimes friends find themselves in awkward situations and they don't know how to act or respond. For example, when your best friend starts to spend a lot of time with a new friend. That's OK. Don't be possessive, they are allowed to have as many friends as they want. That does not mean they care less for you. People should have many friends, the more the better. People evolve and grow through friendships. You too will evolve and change as you meet new people that will aid in your growth and development. Therefore, you should always welcome new friends as they will teach you things about yourself and about life. When your best friend meets a new friend, chances are you will like them too, if you give them a chance. Get to know them. They will probably be another best friend.

Another uncomfortable situation is when both friends like the same person. OMG, this one is difficult and must be handled carefully. You and your best friend must talk this one out and decide who will go for it (If the other person has not already decided who they like between the two of you). There will be one of you that probably met that person first; let that person go for it. If all of you met at the same time, take the time to see who is more compatible. Once a couple is formed, the remaining single friend should step back and let the relationship flourish. Do not take it personally! This means this person was not the one for you. Just know your sweetheart is still out there looking for you too.

There may come a time when you begin feeling an attraction to your best friend's ex. I personally would not go there. Once your best friend dates someone, that person should be off limits to you even if they are not together anymore. It's just distasteful and a bit incestuous. Most people feel awkward in that situation because there are always feelings involved. Your best friend might

Best Friends

feel hurt over the break-up or have unresolved feelings. Or worse, maybe the ex secretly still has feelings for your best friend. Your best friend may want nothing to do with his ex or to see her ever again. In this last case you will not be able to go out with your new sweetheart and your best friend together, ever! In any case, ask your best friend. She might not care. But remember, there is always the chance that your new love/best friend's ex might still have feelings for your best friend and you will never know! Your best friend will always be around you and therefore around them. It will be a very uncomfortable situation and you might lose your best friend over it. Remember, lovers come and go, but true friends are forever.

If your so-called best friend flirts or hits on your sweetie, then she is not your friend and never was. She is thinking about herself and not about you or your feelings. She definitely does not have your back and cannot be trusted. Continuing a friendship with someone like that is a friendship at your own risk. You are better off getting rid of that trash and opening yourself up to a true best friend.

Grown-Ups

"My heroes are and were my parents. I can't see having anyone
else as my heroes."
~ Michael Jordan

Rules, rules, rules and more rules. I know some of you feel like
some rules are unnecessary. But actually, they are not!
Remember, even though you feel you know everything there is to
know right now, believe me, you don't. It is impossible. You are
a new human, growing, evolving and maturing. You still need the
experience of your parents to survive out in the world. You
cannot possibly know all the things that could happen out there in
different scenarios.

Your parents have more life experience and probably know
what to do! Even though it is hard for you to believe and picture,
your parents were once teenagers just like you who felt the same
way you are feeling right now. Chances are they wanted to do the
same things you want to do right now. They learned either from
other people's mistakes, from their own or from experience
passed down from family members or friends. Now, they want to

pass that knowledge down to you, their baby. They just want to protect you because they love you. To them, you are the most important thing in the world. Even if they do not show it in a way you understand. But believe me, you are! You are a little piece of them and they want to protect you as best as they can. You are their treasure and their pride and joy!

When you are not sure about something, ask a trusted grown-up. Chances are they already went through what you are struggling with or know someone who did. Common scenarios: the guy you like is going to be at the party, concert, or whatever and you cannot go because it will be after your curfew; the outfit or thing you just have to have because if you don't you will look like a loser in front of your friends; the broken heart; the people picking on you or bullying you and what would happen if you tell…you feel you will be singled out; sexual peer pressures, drug peer pressure, pregnancy, etc. It is old news. Your generation is not the only one going through these things. These have been going on since the beginning of time! It is human nature. Grown-ups have already gone through all that and know how it feels and how you are feeling right now. Talk to them and tell them what you are going through and how you feel. Remind them how it was for them. They are a great source of life experience and they are there at your disposal. Communicate with your parents, guardian, counselor, or favorite family member; they just want the best for you and for you not to make irreparable mistakes that you will regret for the rest of your life. Listen, get advice, be smart and do the right thing.

Remember, some decisions will have irreversible consequences. A pregnancy, an addiction, a life changing disease, a terminal disease, a criminal record, jail or death are some of the consequences of bad decisions. Grown-ups have dealt with some of these before. Some have made the right decisions at the moment and others learned from their mistakes and are now paying the consequences. This is why grown-ups have rules. To keep you safe and to spare you from making irreversible mistakes that will make your life difficult by having responsibilities too early in life that will hamper your growth and development or just end your life early. Remember, rules come from a place of true love.

Grades

"There are advantages to being elected President. The day after I was elected, I had my high school grades classified Top Secret."
~ Ronald Reagan

You are not totally a fully developed human. Just like wolves and their cubs. The cubs have to be taught to hunt, the rules of the pack and how to stay away from danger until they are ready to be on their own. You are the same, and how we humans teach our cubs is by sending them to school while we go and earn a living to pay for the cave and the food that feeds you, the cub. Now, your job and responsibility is to learn and to be the best human you can be. The grown-ups' responsibility is to protect you, feed you, love you, teach you what you don't learn in school, and provide a conducive environment for you to develop and grow healthy. You've got to keep up with the rest of the pack. It is your responsibility to learn the very basics, which correspond to grades 0-12, then choose your position in the pack, or in human terms, your career and your position as a productive member of society.

If you need help with homework, ask! Ask your friends, parents, teachers or guardians. There are many tutoring services around. Ask your teacher about tutoring after school. Seek the help you need; most brilliant scholars did at one point or another! Don't be left behind, be strong and keep up with the pack. Be a proactive, resourceful and capable human being. Seek the help you need to keep up, now. Remember, time passes by quickly. This is your time to learn, do not leave it for later. Don't get left behind by your friends or classmates. It is harder studying when you are older, really hard. Grown-ups that go to college usually also work and have families who rely on them to meet their basic needs. It is very difficult to go to school when you are working because you will not have any free time. Grown-ups sacrifice to go to school either because they did not have the opportunity to go when they were young or slacked off and now realized the mistake. This is YOUR time to learn! Now! You have the opportunity now while you are young. Take it. Study and learn what you need to learn. Ask for help if you need it. Don't get left behind. Be strong. Keep up with the pack and remember your whole financial success depends a great deal on your education.

Secrets

"The man who can keep a secret may be wise, but he is not half as wise as the man with no secrets to keep."

~ Edgar Watson Howe

Innocent little secrets that don't hurt anyone are fun and they build trust and a bond between friends. You can giggle and laugh amongst yourselves about your little secret and only you know about it. But sometimes secrets can hurt someone physically or emotionally. Secrets can also be dangerous if you don't tell a grown-up. Here are some secrets that should <u>not</u> be kept:

1. If you know that one of your friends is experimenting with drugs: You need to talk to them and tell them the consequences of using drugs. If they don't listen, you can send an anonymous letter to their parents about what your friend is doing. Just sign the note as "a concerned friend." Your friend has taken a dangerous and destructive path that can hurt many people and possibly cost somebody their life.

2. If you know of someone that has been sexually assaulted: You need to talk to them to encourage them to talk to a grown-up or with the authorities. It is extremely dangerous if the attacker is not reported because they may do it again! This is a criminal act of violence and the attacker needs to be removed from society immediately. Even if the attacker is a teenager, they need help before their impulses escalate seeking higher and higher levels of stimulation that can culminate in taking someone's life!

Shhhh

3. If you know of a friend that is doing something that is just wrong: Tell a trusted grown-up, a parent or a teacher. Remember you can do it anonymously. They can try to help your friend and she/he doesn't ever have to find out who reported it. Do it for your friend before they or someone else gets hurt. You would be doing the right thing.

Sexuality

"Boys and girls in America have such a sad time together; sophistication demands that they submit to sex immediately without proper preliminary talk. Not courting talk — real straight talk about souls, for life is holy and every moment is precious."
~ Jack Kerouac

The body is an amazing machine and it is able to reproduce before the brain is fully mature. What does that mean? Well, it means that your body is able to create life before you can fully handle the responsibilities of being a parent and the emotions of being sexually active. Teen years are the years when you should be learning about yourself, what you like and what you don't like, how you respond in certain situations, the careers you are inclined to practice, your talents, traveling and getting to know the world, different cultures and all the wonders out there; the years where you learn about yourself and go through experiences that will make you a well-rounded individual.

I have friends that as they got older they could not understand why they dated the people they dated back when they were teenagers. That's because they were not fully mature yet. The people you date in your teen years sometimes will not be your type once you become an adult. Parents are a good indicator; if your parents don't like him chances are you won't like him either when you get older and more mature. Of course, you might not think so now, but don't make any permanent or life changing decisions now in your teen years such as having a baby, dropping out of school, or getting married. You are still developing and growing and your brain is not yet fully developed. According to Ruben C. Gur, Ph. D., from the University of Pennsylvania, the human brain does not fully mature until the age of 21 or 22.* What this means is that in the adolescent brain, the areas associated with strategy development and decision making are not fully developed. So, teens should not be making any life changing or permanent decisions.

If you are sexually active the best advice for you is abstinence. Do not have sex until you are older and can emotionally handle a sexual relationship, its responsibilities and consequences. Otherwise, if you are sexually active, by all means use protection, but be aware that condoms DO break and the pill is used to prevent you from getting pregnant NOT from catching a sexually transmitted disease. So there are still substantial risks of

Sexuality

contracting a sexually transmitted disease or ending up with an unwanted pregnancy.

Be aware that you can still catch a sexually transmitted disease by having other forms of sexual contact. There are lots of sexually transmitted diseases out there and you cannot tell by looking at a person if they are sick or not. They might not even have any symptoms or know that they are sick! Some sexually transmitted diseases can cause very uncomfortable symptoms and health complications for the rest of your life such as blindness or even death. The best way to protect yourself is through abstinence, or waiting to be sexually active until you are older. If you wait until you are mentally and emotionally ready to handle a sexual relationship, your will be more apt to choose a partner that has been as careful as you and has only been in committed relationships, not sleeping around with everyone they meet.

For now, you should be getting to know lots of people, making lots of friends, preparing for your future, getting some culture by traveling and just enjoying your youth.

Now, let's address homosexuality. If you find yourself attracted to the same sex be aware that sometimes this is a phase for some teens. But if you have had these feeling all your life and feel you are in fact gay do not get depressed over this. Talk to your counselor or parents, or have your parents take you to a professional who specializes in "teen homosexuality" so that you can get advice on how to deal with the lifestyle and society. There are many organizations out there that help gay teens.** Contact them if you need help.

> "Those who mind don't matter, and those who matter don't mind."
> ~ Bernard M. Baruch

Always know that there is absolutely nothing wrong with you. You are a normal, precious, beautiful and unique human being. Humans come in many colors and flavors and we are all different. DO NOT let anyone make you feel otherwise. Not everyone is evolved enough to accept people who are different from who they are. If you encounter these people, do NOT talk about your sexuality with them, or if you can, do not hang around them at all. You have to be safe and must create a positive world around you. Only hang around people you know, for a fact, care about you and don't care about your sexuality. If you meet a new person online or someone from school wants to date you, make sure you meet him with a group of friends and NEVER meet him alone, at least until you and your friends get to know him better. This is a very important safety precaution. Also, always go places in your car or

48

a trusted friend's car. NEVER EVER get in the car of someone you've just met or met recently!

Surround yourself with people who love you for who you are and treasure you just the way you are, beautiful and unique you.

*Read more at:

http://www.americanbar.org/content/dam/aba/publishing/criminal_justice_s
ection_newsletter/crimjust_juvjus_Adolescence.authcheckdam.pdf
** Organizations that offer assistance to gay and lesbians

1. Affirmations – Help for gays and lesbians. Phone: 1-800-398-GAYS
Website:
http://www.goaffirmations.org/site/PageServer?pagename=programs_helpline
2.   GLBT – Gay, Lesbian, Bisexual and Transgender Hot Line.
GLBT National Hotline: 1-888-843-4564
GLBT National Youth Talk Line: 1-800-246-7743
Online Peer Chat Support Website: http://www.glnh.org/talkline/index.html
3.   GLAAD - The Gay & Lesbian Alliance Against Defamation
Website: http://www.glaad.org
4. PFLAG – Parents, Family of Lesbians and Gays
Website: http://community.pflag.org/Page.aspx?pid=194&srcid=-2

Siblings

"A brother is a friend given by Nature."

~ Jean Baptiste Legouve

Siblings are a blessing for most of us. These people will be with us for the rest of our lives through difficult and happy times. They are our blood; therefore you should always try to get along. Follow these rules for a happy home:

- Focus on the things you have in common with your sibling and shy away from the things you don't.
- Show them that you care by being there for them in times of need.

"THE MILDEST, DROWSIEST SISTER HAS BEEN KNOWN TO TURN TIGER IF HER SIBLING IS IN TROUBLE" ~ CLARA ORTEGA

- Keep secrets unless those secrets put your sibling in danger. Such as using drugs, hanging with the wrong crowd and engaging in illegal activities. If you have to tell on them, do it anonymously so your trust is not broken.

- Respect your sibling and their property. DO NOT take their belongings without asking.

- If they lend you something, return it in the same shape it was given to you and when you agreed to return it. This creates trust.

- If you have different personalities and find it difficult to get along, still respect your sibling, DO NOT call her names. Once you go down that road you will create an uncomfortable environment for you and your family in your home that will be very difficult to change.

- Be respectful and keep it light. You want to keep or create a loving and comfortable environment in your home.

- Try to talk things out calmly and don't point fingers. Start the conversation with, "I wish I could get my stuff back when I was promised," or "I wish we would get along better; you know I do love you." You will not believe how good that would sound to them even if they don't show it right now. Or if you find it difficult talking to them in person, write them a note! Make sure you sign, "love you."

- When angry take a walk, a deep breath, listen to your music or whatever works for you. DO NOT get into a fight. Some fights are unforgivable and you cannot take back things that you say when you get angry. This will make your home life tense and uncomfortable. So say "I'm sorry" if it was your fault or just get away for a while until things cool off.

- Be polite, remember you have to live with your siblings. So be respectful and polite to get the same back.

- Show your sibling you care and love her. Buy her favorite candy or something she likes when you go out.

- Surprise your sibling and invite him out. Take him to do what you guys have in common like an arcade, a baseball practice cage, bowling, or to the mall.

- Don't compete. Your sibling may have things that she's good at, but you have other things you are good at. If you don't know what, find them! Embrace the beautiful and unique you.

- Help your sister if she's going through a rough time. You

are going to need her help one day.

- Always stand up for family in school. These are the people you live with and they are going to be around for the rest of your life. So support your siblings against anyone. One day you may be the one who needs help.

- Copying or imitation is a form of flattery. If your little sister copies everything you do, don't get irritated; she thinks you are great and she wants to be just like you! It's truly a compliment!

Remember, friends and boyfriends may come and go, but family and siblings are forever. You don't have to hang with your sibling, but you do want to live in a comfortable and loving environment so make sure they know you love them and then move on to your friends and other things.

Bullying

"Courage is fire, and bullying is smoke."

~ Benjamin Disraeli

Bullying is wrong and it can have grave consequences. The "Universal Rule" tells us we should treat others as we want to be treated. There is **NO** excuse for one human being to do harm to another human being. It is just wrong!

All of these are considered forms of bullying: physical bullying, emotional bullying, cyber bullying and sexting, or circulating suggestive, nude photos or messages about a person.

> The Golden Rule:
> "Treat Others as
> You Want to Be
> Treated."

At least half of all suicides among young people are related to bullying, according to a recent study released in Britain. Studies conducted by Yale University also found bullying victims are between two to nine times more likely to consider suicide than non-victims. The following are known cases of suicide due to some form of bullying:

- Sixteen-year-old Gary Hansen who hanged himself in Roblin, Man. Canada, after persistent bullying at his local high school. (1)

- In another suicide case, the prosecutor brought charges against six teenagers claiming that their taunting and physical threats led Phoebe Prince to hang herself from a stairwell. (2)

- Eric Mohat, 17, was harassed and bullied so badly that he did not have the strength to go on anymore and when he was told by his bully to go home and shoot himself, he did! (3)

- Hope Witsell, 13, sent a topless picture of herself to a boy hoping to get his attention and instead the picture was spread all over her school and the local high school. Hope Witsell could not bear the embarrassment and hanged herself. (4)

- Eighteen-year-old Jesse Logan killed herself when an ex-boyfriend forwarded explicit photos of her after they ended their relationship. (5)

- Thirteen-year-old Asher Brown committed suicide after being the target of anti-gay bullying. (6)

If you do a keyword search on Google using "suicide due to bullying" you will find many victims who committed suicide because they could not take the bullying anymore.

Bullying is an action that can also result in violence. When the victim has had enough they can also retaliate; under duress you cannot be sure how that person will react. The Columbine massacre may have been related to bullying since the shooters had been victims of bullying in the past. You don't know how the person you are picking on will react. You don't know her or his mental state and you certainly do not want to be responsible for their death or maybe yours and others!

If you are dealing with anger issues and engage in bullying, seek help before you hurt someone. Don't pass your anger to someone else, who in turn, may hurt other people. Bullying spreads hate, it doesn't stop with your victim. The person you bullied may turn around and abuse the next person they come into contact with because you angered them and now they are in a bad mood because of you. They may bully someone smaller than them. You will be spreading hate and violence and you never know it may come full circle back to you. You don't know how far your actions will go or how many people will be affected or hurt. Instead, aim for one good deed a day and when they thank you, tell that person to just pass it on. You will be surprised how far your chain reaction of good deeds will go and how many people will benefit from your kindness. You never know, it may come back to you.

Think of how you want to be remembered. Do you want to be remembered as an abuser who took advantage of the weak and was responsible for a chain reaction of hate and violence or a great human being who helped humanity by helping those less fortunate and a good friend who made the world a better place by standing up for the weak and less fortunate? Do your best to spread good deeds and good will, not hate and violence, and you will make the world a better place.

If you are being bullied seek help immediately. Talk to your parents, teacher or counselor. If you are having suicidal thoughts or feelings like you want to hurt someone please seek help. Talk to your parents and let them know you need to talk to a professional. Please do so before it is too late. There are many organizations out there that can help you by connecting you to another teen or a professional for free such as:

Bullying

Teen Line http://teenlineonline.org/

Teen Contact http://www.teencontact.org/

Love is Respect http://www.loveisrespect.org/

(1) http://www.cbc.ca/news/background/bullying

(2) http://www.nytimes.com/2010/03/30/us/30bully.html

(3) http://abcnews.go.com/Health/MindMoodNews/story?id=7228335

(4) http://today.msnbc.msn.com/id/34236377/ns/today-today_people/t/sexting-bullying-cited-teens-suicide/

(5) http://www2.nbc4i.com/news/2012/may/15/jessica-logan-anti-bullying-act-signed-law-ar-1037734/

(6) http://www.cbsnews.com/8301-504763_162-20019163-10391704.html

Careers and Your Future

"Everybody is a genius. But if you judge a fish by its ability to climb a tree, it will live its whole life believing that it is stupid."

~ Albert Einstein

This is something parents should talk about with their children early. I cannot emphasize this enough. The sooner you start to think about your future and what career you want to study the better chance you will have at success. Some of the most successful people were exposed to their careers early in life. Either they already had a passion for something and knew what they wanted to be, or their parents exposed them early on to their future career. After that, they practiced and practiced and practiced some more. Today, these people are experts in their fields making the big bucks. Here are a few of them:

- **Steven Spielberg** in his teen years started to make amateur 8 mm "adventure" films with his friends, the first of which he shot at the Pinnacle Peak Patio restaurant in

Scottsdale. He charged .25 cents admission to his home films, which involved the wrecks he staged with his Lionel train set while his sister sold popcorn. Spielberg began his career at Universal Studios as an unpaid intern and guest of the editing department.

- **Tiger Woods** started playing and practicing golf when he was just two years old!

- Pop singer/songwriter **Tori Amos** began to play the piano by age two. By age five, she had begun composing instrumental pieces on piano!

- **Oprah Winfrey** played games interviewing her corncob doll and the crows on the fence of her family's property as a child. As a teenager, she started a part-time job at a local radio station, WVOL, where she reported the news. (1) Winfrey worked there during her senior year of high school and again while in her first two years of college.

- **Isaac Newton** discovered the generalized binomial theorem and began to develop a mathematical theory that later became infinitesimal calculus at age 18! Calculus is the basic mathematical operation used by computers. We owe our current digital age pretty much to Newton.

My point is that to be successful it takes practice. The earliest you figure out what you are passionate about or where your talents lie, the more years you have to practice and the better you will become at your career. This translates into better chances at success, which in turn, means lots of money and freedom to do what you want to do. Don't waste time. Start early and delve into

Careers and Your Future

different career options. Some fun and interesting career options are sports, music, mathematics, science, fashion, reporting, biology, flying or healthcare. The best place to start is to take the Myers Briggs personality test. (2) Then head over to salary.com and check out the salaries of the careers that came up in your Myers Briggs personality test. You can also search on salary.com under a specific career area and see all the different options you have and their salaries. Don't limit yourself to the obvious careers; there are careers out there that you have likely never heard of before. Once you discover your talent, your passion, or perfect career path investigate everything about it and start to immerse yourself in everything related to that field. Take classes in school or make an appointment to shadow a professional to see if that's what you really like. Get an internship and practice, practice, practice. There is no time to waste, the earlier you start the better! Remember, the world is very competitive so the more experience you have and the better prepared you are the better chances you have against people competing with you for the same position.

Use your time wisely! Enjoy your teen years, but also practice and prepare for the future. Don't be left behind by your successful peers.

Teen Life

(1) Lee Winfrey, "Praise from All Corners for New Talk Show Host", *Syracuse Herald Journal*, September 9, 1986, p. 44

(2) http://www.humanmetrics.com/cgi-win/jtypes2.asp

Money

"If you would know the value of money, go and try to borrow some."

~ Benjamin Franklin

Everybody needs some. You probably need some right now for a car, music, clothes, dating, to buy video games and that cool looking cell phone or gadget. There are many ways you can acquire some funds. In case you cannot think of any that would work for you, here some easy ways to get money:

1. Ask your parents if you can do some chores around the house for pay.
2. Ask your neighbors if they have any chores you can do such as mowing their lawns.
3. Get a part-time job at the mall, movie theater, as a lifeguard, the local pizza place, hotel, resort, amusement park, camp, museum, ranch, as a driver, a ski instructor, a river guide, or whatever job is open that you can do

successfully. Check out coolworks.com for great jobs in great places. You can also search for part-time jobs at careerbuilders.com.

4. If you are good with selling stuff on eBay, open an eBay broker business and put flyers in your neighborhood offering to sell your neighbor's stuff for a percentage.

5. Become a photographer and sell your photos online.

6. Tutor other teens for a fee.

7. If you are good at Photoshop offer to design logos or illustrations for businesses.

8. Find cool items at garage sales and sell them on eBay.

9. Run an errand service business.

10. Are you good with dogs? Get a book on dog training and open your own dog training business.

11. Open a dog walking business.

12. Got a driver's license? Offer to be a driver for senior citizens.

13. Love animals? Apply at your local zoo.

14. Get a job at your local newspaper delivering newspapers.

15. Are you good with kids? Be a babysitter.

16. Open a house painting business.

17. Great with computers? Offer computer classes or help.

As you can see, there are lots of options you just have to be creative. If you see a need you can fulfill then that is your opportunity!

Once you have some funds, open a checking account. Try to get a checking account that pays interest so you can earn money on the money you deposit in the bank. There is also something called compound interest which is great for your wallet. It means you open an account that pays interest and leave that money there to grow. You will get paid a percentage of your balance every month or every year, depending on your bank. That means that your interest will be added to the balance on your account. So, the next time the bank pays interest again, it will be based on your total balance including the interest that was added the last time and so on every month! So your money will multiply!

If you need a resume, replace the information below with your own. The following résumé is for a recent high school graduate with no work experience:

Money

Name
123 Some Street

Anytown, CA 00000

Telephone

Email

Achievements

Member of ABC Honor Society, high school honor roll. Listed on the Dean's List 2012. President of Student Government. Member of the Debate Team.

Education

2009 – 2012   South Miami High School, Miami, Florida

2001 – 2098   Hill Elementary School, Miami, Florida

Skills

Proficient with Microsoft Word, Excel, and PowerPoint, and Java Types 60 wpm.

Teen Life

Extra-Curricular Activities

Runner's Club

Volunteering at DEF Homeless Shelter

Tutor

References

John Smith	Teacher	543-000-0000
Bob Johnston	Teacher	543-000-0000
Dan Hall	Coach	543-000-0000

Money

The following résumé is for a teen with some work experience:

Name

123 Some Street

Anytown, CA 00000

Telephone

Email

Achievements

Member of ABC Honor Society, high school honor roll. Listed on the Dean's List 2012. President of Student Government. Member of the Debate Team.

Education

2009 – 2012   South Miami High School, Miami, Florida

2001 – 2098   Hill Elementary School, Miami, Florida

Skills

Proficient with Microsoft Word, Excel, and PowerPoint, and Java Types 60 wpm.

Teen Life

Extra-Curricular Activities

Runner's Club

Volunteering at DEF Homeless Shelter

Tutor

Experience

Office Assistant, **FIU**, Miami, Florida

Summer 2011 - Present

- Coordinated appointments
- Answer phones
- Made travel arrangements

Cashier, **Fast Supermarket**, Southampton, PA

Fall 2010 - 2011

- Was selected employee of the month for efficient, friendly service
- Promoted to Office Assistant in September, 2010

Now go! Be a productive member of society and start earning!

Nobody Understands

"The whole secret of existence is to have no fear. Never fear what will become of you, depend on no one. Only the moment you reject all help are you freed."

~ Buddha

You will be surprised how many people out there DO understand. If you talked to someone and they did not understand or relate, keep looking until you find someone who has gone through what you are going through or a professional that has the expertise to help and give you advice.

There are many people you can talk to such as counselors at your school, a teacher, your parents, a trusted minister, a family member, a friend or an organization that helps people in your situation. Just find someone who can help. Here are some organizations that offer assistance to teens:

1. Teen Line - teenlineonline.org - 1-800-852-8336
2. Teencentral.net

3. United States National Suicide & Crisis Hotlines: This site gives hotline numbers based on your area and they also list other national hotlines.

http://suicidehotlines.com/national.html

Remember the world is very old and there are billions of people out there. Chances are that there are lots of people out there that have experienced what you are going through and they seek out teens that they can help and advise. There are always resources out there and people willing to help. Remember, nothing lasts forever, everything eventually must come to an end, and time DOES heal. What I'm trying to say is, if you are feeling the situation is hopeless, or there is no way out, or it hurts so much that it is impossible to feel better, eventually with time you WILL feel better. There are many people out there that have felt the same thing you are feeling right now and they offer help to people that are going through what they went through because they already know how it feels, what helped them and that in time it WILL get better. So seek out people and organizations who offer help. Accept the help you need right now to help you cope and soon you will be on the road to happiness again.

If you are contemplating suicide, by all means talk to your parents, teacher or school counselor. You can call The National Suicide Prevention Lifeline at 1-800-273-8255 to get help. Even if it seems to you like there is no hope, please believe there IS hope and there is help out there that can make you feel better. You just have to be strong and resilient and find the perfect help for you that will make you feel great again.

Difficult People

"Difficult People are your key to self-empowerment, you need to learn how to cope with them, not let them dominate and affect you."

~ Janice Davies

There are always some people that stand out by being mean, obnoxious or just plain difficult. The best way to deal with these people is not to deal with them at all! Stay as far away from them as possible. You don't need that negative energy around you.

If you are being bullied, read the chapter titled, "Bullying" to help you learn how to handle a bully. If someone is spreading rumors about you:

1. Tell your parents and have them contact that child's parent or the school.

2. Bring evidence to your school's attention. Such as Facebook prints or whatever evidence you can get to show authorities. Today, most schools have implemented ways to deal with such problems.

3. Ignore it. Act happy like it does not bother you at all. Have a "who Cares?" or a "so what?" attitude. If they see it doesn't bother you, they will eventually stop.

4. They are doing this to get a reaction out of you. Do not give them the pleasure. Hang around people who truly know and love you. Have fun and continue your life ignoring the rumors. When they see that their evil rumors have not impacted your life, they will stop.

5. You can send an anonymous letter to the guidance counselor and turn the evil person in. You might want to include proof like her Facebook account link. In some schools, they will get suspended for posting inappropriate statements on Facebook or any social network.

6. If you feel comfortable enough to confront the rumor, you can fight it by telling your side of the story and letting people know the reason why this person is spreading the rumors. Jealousy or envy is usually the reason. Just let your friends know what a loser he or she is by being jealous or envious. Be sure to mention that they should get their own life instead of being so fascinated with yours! Really! Tell your real friends to help by telling others that the rumors are not true and the reason why they are being spread is just jealousy or envy. Pretty soon the tables will be turned on the person spreading the rumors and they will look like the fool. Why are they so fascinated with you, right?

7. This is a no-brainer, but I'm going to mention it just in case. Do NOT hang with the person spreading the rumors. They are not your friend and obviously do not have your best interests at heart. If you are seen hanging with the person spreading the rumors, people will assume the rumors are true. Duh.

8. You can confront the person and ask them to prove it. Granted that the rumor is not true.

If some girl is just mean to you ignore her. Don't let her see you sweat. Laugh and be happy and eventually she will leave you alone. Don't let her see you upset. Show her that she does not have control over your life or how you feel. Pretend you don't even hear her. Ignoring them is the best weapon.

ⅅrugs

"Drugs are a waste of time. They destroy your memory and your self-respect and everything that goes along with your self-esteem."
~ Kurt Cobain

This one should be a no-brainer, but I will talk about it none the less. Drugs are harmful in so many ways. They damage your body and mind and hurt the people around you, your community, and your country...really! Let me explain, in case you don't see how.

Drugs are addictive and almost impossible to quit and usually lead to harsher drugs. As you become addicted, you are going to need a higher high every time. This means you are going to need more money to spend on more drugs. If you don't stop at this point you can die from a drug overdose.

Drugs have everlasting effects. Once you let that drug into your body it damages and changes your brain chemistry forever. Your thinking may never be the same, your memory will be affected, and you might develop a tick, or become more

Drugs

aggressive. In short, your brain will be changed and less effective. In this competitive world you are going to need all your brain neurons and then some to be able to compete and make a decent living. Remember, you will be competing with other people for assignments, promotions or jobs. You better be sharp.

Drugs lead to violence and death. Since they are illegal, lives are lost while attempting to transport the drugs. Dealers often kill other dealers competing in their territory and children and other innocent people have been shot in drug-related drive by shootings. Some people have been mugged, including myself, and/or killed by addicts trying to get money for their next fix. Elderly people have been killed by drug addicts looking for money. In addition, many women have been raped by drug addicts who were high at the time, children have been kidnapped over drugs, and some children have been left orphans due to drug-related crimes. Just search the internet for drug related violence and get more informed. By buying drugs you will be sponsoring and contributing to all these crimes, acts of violence and the deaths of innocent people and children.

If you are approached by a friend offering you drugs, this person is NOT your friend. Here are a few reasons why they are offering you drugs:

1. They want you to get addicted to make money off of you, selling you the drug later.
2. They want you to get addicted so that you will buy the drug sometimes and share because it is hard for them to get the money on their own.
3. They don't like being the only loser taking drugs. Misery loves company.
4. Or they just want you to get addicted and look like a loser.

Remember, the majority of people who use drugs either end up in jail or dead. The ones that escape death or jail quit using drugs before it got out of hand. Imagine you are young and meet your sweetheart and get married. You both work hard to create your life, buy a home and have babies. You treasure your babies. They are a part of you; a little person you brought into the world. A mini you! You love your baby and want the best for him. The baby is so sweet and hugs you so tight. He stretches his little arms and chubby little fingers for you to pick him up. You love your baby so much and he loves you back. You watch him grow and learn. Then he starts using drugs. His personality changes, he hates you now, he steals from you, and he is getting violent. How would you feel? Most parents are devastated and get so stressed out over the situation that they develop diseases or medical conditions and some even lose their jobs! Family will be affected and shamed. Their kid did not win a scholarship; he doesn't have a promising future. Instead, he is the addict that breaks into neighbors' homes for money; the one who has a very good chance of becoming an inmate or dying!

Drugs are NOT manufactured in clean labs, nor are those places regulated to make sure the manufactured drugs do not actually harm you. The labs are usually dirty and run in deplorable conditions. Drugs are sometimes manufactured by addicts themselves. You don't know how the drug was manufactured, if it is the right mixture, or who touched the drug. People have died just from the wrong mixture of chemicals to make the drug.

If you have a friend that is using, the best thing you can do is send an anonymous letter to his or her parents and stay away from them. Drug users are no longer thinking clearly, and guess what? If they get in trouble while you are hanging with them, you are going to get in trouble too. Authorities will assume you are also using drugs.

Find new friends, people who are actually going somewhere in life and will help you succeed. Hanging with drug users is a threat to your freedom and possibly your life.

There have been instances where the person using drugs has been hanging at their friend's house when drug dealers have busted in the house demanding their money. At that time the only thing the drug dealers are thinking about is getting their money back. They don't care if they hurt you or kill anyone in the process. So hanging around with people who are using drugs is extremely dangerous.

Most drugs are not manufactured in your area. They come from other states or even other countries. This means tax dollars have to be spent protecting and policing borders, instead of other programs that will help citizens have a better life or other programs to make our country great. Helium has been popping up in parties recently. Although it is fun to listen to your own voice sounding like the voice of a mouse, helium in sufficient concentration – directly from a tank for example – crowds out the oxygen in your body and can kill you. That's what happened to 14-year-old Ashley Long. (1)

When there is a lot of drug violence, your state needs to invest in more protection in the form of police officers. Their police officers' salaries come from the taxes people pay. More crime, more officers and more taxes you have to pay; sometimes in the form of property taxes. So instead of using the money toward more productive things for the community like creating parks, programs for the elderly, the homeless, the needy, children, schools or beautifying your city, the money goes to fight drug related crime.

(1) http://www.cbsnews.com/8301-504083_162-57383982-504083/14-year-old-oregon-girl-dies-after-inhaling-helium-at-party/

$\mathcal{P}$eer $\mathcal{P}$ressures

"I'm not in this world to live up to your expectations and you're not in this world to live up to mine."

~ Bruce Lee

Some peer pressures are actually good because they will motivate you to be more productive. For example: Your friends are getting good grades and since you don't want to be the idiot of the group, you try to study harder to make your grades match theirs.

Your friend just got this cool jacket or gadget. OMG, it is so cool. And they have money to buy all this cool stuff and money to go out. You don't want to feel left behind; you want to have money too! So you get your first job. Now you have money too.

If you hang around high achievers, or people who are productive and going places, it will rub off on you. Soon you will feel motivated to achieve more.

On the other hand, some peer pressures such as the pressures to have sex, use drugs, drink alcohol or commit criminal activity are dangerous and deadly. If you go along with these peer pressures, be aware that eventually you will get caught. You may catch a sexually transmitted disease, get pregnant, end up in jail or worse dead.

Other peer pressures, if you are weak, can lead you to actions that can be dangerous or have negative consequences for the rest of your life. Sex can have consequences that will stay with you for the rest of your life. You can end up dealing with a nasty disease for the rest of your life, if it doesn't kill you. And how embarrassing it will be, once you are older to tell your sweetheart that you have a sexually transmitted disease that you have to deal with for the rest of your life? Read the chapter "Sexuality."

A pregnancy when you are too young can seriously make your life extremely difficult. You will need more money for babysitting so that you can continue your education and get a career that pays enough money to take care for your child. You will need someone to take care of your baby every three hours when she is crying because she will need to be fed, changed, scratched, moved or just played with so that you can continue to sleep. Without sleep, how else can you work up the energy you need to get up and go to school the next day? You will also need a babysitter or someone that will be willing to give up their own personal free time to take care of your baby when you want to go out. It will be YOUR baby so it will be YOUR responsibility to deal with the late night feedings, diaper changes and spats of crying. No one should give up their saved and hard earned money and time to relax to take care of what YOU created.

Drugs and alcohol can scar you for life, hurt your loved ones, or kill you. You can damage your brain to the point where it doesn't process information as fast as it should. You will be slower in your thinking processes and in this competitive world you need all your brain cells to successfully compete and succeed.

Drugs are addictive, sometimes from the first try, which means your life will consist of trying to find money to buy more drugs. It won't matter if you have to steal or hurt someone; you need your next fix. No more fun and no more future. Really pathetic. And if you don't stop, you might overdose since you need more and more of the drug each time to get the same high. You could go to prison for possession of an illegal narcotic and with a criminal record that will make it almost impossible to get a decent paying job and forget about a career. Be aware that good places to work require a drug test to be hired and random drug tests later on. So if you want to be successful stay away from drugs.

Be smart. If you feel pressured by some losers to do something you know is wrong, feel sorry for them because they are going down the wrong path and remove yourself fast from their company. Your true friends want the best for you and will never ask you to do something that can make your life difficult, make you sick, land you in jail or kill you.

Teen Pregnancy

"Reducing teen pregnancy and birth is one of the most effective ways of reducing child poverty in the country."

~ Jordan Brown

Pregnancy can be a blessing at the right time or disastrous at the wrong time. When pregnancy happens in the teen years, it is extremely difficult for the family and the teen parents – that is, IF the teen father even sticks around. This stressful time affects the baby, as well as your relationships with the teen father and your family. Fun times with your boyfriend will be over. The excitement of dating, going out and carefree fun with your boyfriend will turn into responsibilities, such as working after school, and you will hardly have time to spend with your boyfriend anymore. Your time will be dedicated to school, work and your baby. Your money will now go to a babysitter, baby clothes, baby medical bills, baby food, college expenses for your child just to name a few. No more money for clothes, going out or spring vacations, and you will be lucky if you can save for a car, or put money away for emergencies such as medical and car repairs. No more going out late since your baby needs to eat every three hours and after that you need to play with him, give him love and reassurance, and put him to sleep again. You will need to check his diaper frequently because if you don't he can get sick and develop skin disorders. Check out this article (3) from Babycenter.com to get an idea of what a typical day in the life of a mother and her baby is really like.

Teen Pregnancy

If there is no commitment from the father such as a marriage, there is NO guarantee that he will stick around to help you maintain a home and support your baby. The teen father is just a child himself that has just started to venture out into the world. The odds of him giving up his freedom to assume grown-up responsibilities are slim. The statistics are eight out of ten teen fathers don't marry the mother of their child. (2)

It is careless and selfish to bring a child into such a situation where there is no marriage, careers have not yet been established and extreme financial pressures are put on your parents. Only 40 percent of teens who have children before age 18 actually graduate from high school, compared to 75 percent of teens from similar social and economic backgrounds who do not give birth until ages 20 or 21. (1)   With no professional skills it is almost impossible to find employment. Without a job or career, it will be extremely difficult to take care of yourself and your baby. Statistics also show that about 80 percent of teen mothers end up on welfare and with little hope to get out of poverty. (4)   Children cost money; just remember when you wanted clothes, a cell phone, a car or money to go out. Your child will want those things too. According to the U.S. Department of Agriculture, this is the typical cost to bring up a child:

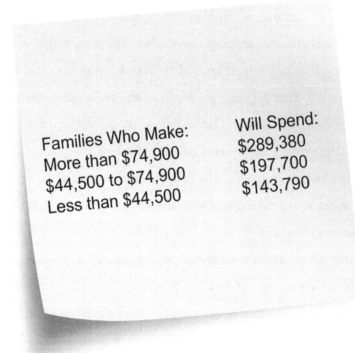

Families Who Make:	Will Spend:
More than $74,900	$289,380
$44,500 to $74,900	$197,700
Less than $44,500	$143,790

You will need a baby sitter if you want to continue your education and they cost money. You cannot possibly expect your parents to give up their much deserved free time after work to take care of your responsibility. It is not fair to them. They already took care of THEIR responsibility, you!

Pregnancy should be the fruit of a committed and mature relationship where both parents live together, have established careers, finances are in order and a child is wanted by both. A child needs the love and support of both parents to grow healthy. Therefore, make sure the baby's father is committed to you before you have a child. By commitment, I mean marriage. Don't make the mistake of thinking that by getting pregnant your boyfriend will stick around; there are many single teen mothers out there to disprove that theory. Like I mentioned earlier, the statistics of teen fathers sticking around is two out of ten, which means eight out of 10 teen fathers won't stay. (2) There are no guarantees that a young boy just starting life and beginning to get a taste of freedom from his parents, is going to settled down to assume the adult responsibilities of raising a child without even getting the chance to venture out in the world or secure a career. He's beginning to hang out with girls, his buddies and to have fun. Boys will rarely want to give up this freedom to settle down and submit to a life of struggle and poverty. They are not emotionally or financially ready for this responsibility so early in life and neither are you.

A baby is a big responsibility. He or she is a new human being that will become an adult and will demand answers one day. You have in your hands the life of a new human being that needs to be cared for the proper way. Babies born to teen mothers are more likely to have a low birth weight, are usually born prematurely – which cause medical problems for the rest of their lives — and are more likely to die within the first year than babies born to older women. (5)

In your teen years, you should be getting to know yourself, meeting new and exciting people, forming life long connections, experiencing life, traveling to foreign lands and getting to know the many different cultures in the world, researching possible careers options that you would enjoy, shadowing professionals, and getting ready for your next stage in life, adulthood.

Teen Pregnancy

Also read: Adolescent Pregnancy in America: Causes and Responses
http://specialpopulations.org/Vol%2030-1%20Chapters/JVSNEVol30-
1_Fall07_Domenico.pdf

(1) http://www.thenationalcampaign.org/costs/pdf/report/6-
BTN_Consequences_for_Parents.pdf
(2) http://drphil.com/articles/article/684
(3) http://www.babycenter.com/0_sample-baby-schedules-for-5-and-6-
month-olds_3657233.bc
(4) http://www.teenhelp.com/teen-pregnancy/consequences-of-teen-
pregnancy-options.html
(5) http://www.thenationalcampaign.org/why-it-matters/pdf/health.pdf

$\mathcal{B}eing\ \mathcal{D}ifferent$

"Be who you are and say what you feel, because those who mind
don't matter and those who matter don't mind."

~ Dr. Seuss

So you think you are different. News flash Einstein, we all are.
No two individuals are the same in the whole world. I know,
somehow you feel really different like you don't belong. Don't
despair, this just means you have not found your group yet.
Believe me, they are out there. Join groups that cater to your
hobbies such as chess, cycling, scuba diving, computers, martial
arts, kick boxing, geocaching or whatever interests you and you
will find people just like you that share your hobbies and make
some new friends along the way. In case you have some form of
physical disability here is a short list of people who overcame
theirs and became successful:

- **Stephen Hawkins**, a renowned physicist who grow up
  with ALS or Lou Gehrig's disease (a motor neuron

disease).

- Olympic 100m hurdles bronze medalist Priscilla **Lopes-Schliep** born with lipodystrophy (a condition characterized by the loss of the subcutaneous fat that helps insulate the body).

- The famous music composer **Ludwig van Beethoven,** who was deaf.

- Famous actor **Tom Cruise** overcame dyslexia.

- **Thomas Edison,** the famous inventor of the practical light bulb overcame dyslexia and deafness.

- **Tommy Hilfiger,** the internationally known fashion designer overcame HD/AD.

- **Justin Timberlake,** famous singer and actor overcame dyslexia and AD/HD.

- Famous singer and actress **Barbara Streisand** overcame a social phobia.

- Professional football player and winner of the Heisman trophy **Ricky Williams** overcame social anxiety.

- **Kim Basinger,** a famous actress, also overcame social anxiety.

- Actor and producer **Bruce Willis** overcame stuttering.

- Actor **Christopher Joseph Burke** has Down syndrome.

- Writer, actor and producer **Dan Ackroyd** was diagnosed with Tourette's and Asperger's syndromes as a teenager.

This is just a small group of well known people who have overcome disabilities and have gone to develop successful careers and lives. If you do an internet search for "famous people with disabilities," you will be surprised at how many overcame theirs and became very successful members of society.

Never give up, keep going forward and do what you have to do to achieve. Find people like you and put yourself out there because you never know, people who you think are not like you, may very well be like you or would like you after they get to know you. Be confident, charming and friendly and you will attract people.

We all feel we are different at one time in our lives. What matters is how you react to those feelings. Do you embrace your uniqueness and grow from there or do you just keep trying to be someone you are not? As you get older, you will begin to appreciate the beautiful and unique person you are and feel more like a part of it all.

Weight and Looking Fabulous

"Everything has beauty, but not everyone sees it."
~ Confucius

All teens feel awkward at one point or another about their bodies. You are growing and will continue to grow until your twenties. Well, some parts of your bodies will continue to grow until old age. The way you look as a teen might not be the way you look as an adult, so don't fret. Boys that are skinny sometimes tend to be tall, strong men and girls that are way too skinny now may grow to have beautiful figures. The point is your body is still growing and changing.

Of course, there are some things you can do now to facilitate a certain body later. Take care of your body by eating the stuff that it needs. Have a balanced diet, exercise and drink plenty of water and not so much sugary sodas. Exercise can be anything that gets your heart rate up and moves your body. Like walking fast, swimming, dancing, tennis, jogging, bicycling, skating; anything that gets you moving. Yoga and Tai Chi are really good for your body too.

If you are having problems with your skin, stop drinking sodas and lower your sugar intake. Over the counter medications work well if you stick to them and use them as directed. I still have a problem with pimples once in a while and I've noticed that using Oxy every other day followed by a face moisturizer will prevent new breakouts. This regimen has worked well for me. Follow the instructions on the box. But be aware that it will dry your skin so after you apply it, apply an oil free face moisturizer that will not clog pores. Soon your face will start to clear up. If after a month of use you don't see an improvement you might have an underlying condition, and it will be best to seek medical advice.

Your diet is very important in your teen years. Since you are growing, you need to give your body the nutrients that it needs for your bones and muscles to grow strong and for your organs to work efficiently. For those of you that need to lose some weight, remember you have to start with a lifestyle change NOT a diet. You have to change the lifestyle that has led you to accumulate the extra pounds. If you had a sedentary lifestyle before, that likely led to the body you have now. If you are not happy with your body then be proactive and change your lifestyle. Pick up a hobby that gets you moving like bicycling, rollerblading, swimming, fast walking, tennis, snorkeling, diving, hiking, mountain biking or anything that gets you moving. Start with setting time aside for your fun activity and get a buddy to join you. Be more active and follow the food plan below. This IS NOT a diet but a lifestyle change! Remember, always get medical advice before a lifestyle change and consult your doctor to make sure there are no underlying conditions that are causing you to gain weight. The following is a plan that worked for me and my friends. It was given to us by our trainer and we got skinny!

While you are in the losing weight stage, these are the things you should not eat:

- Sugar
- Oils
- Dairy
- No Red Meats

Once you lose the weight your doctor recommended you to lose, then you can have these things sparingly. Refined sugar is very addictive; once you have it you will crave it. So be very careful with refined sugar. I started using Stevia which is a natural alternative to sugar and now I'm used to it.

You are going to eat every three to four hours. Never wait more than 4 ½ hours because after that your metabolism will start to slow down. We don't want that. Your metabolism is what burns calories. You need to eat every three to four hours to keep your metabolism going and burning calories.

For those of you who don't eat breakfast, big mistake. Breakfast kick-starts your metabolism in the morning so you burn more fat during the day. When you wake up, you have been without food as many hours as you have been sleeping and your metabolism has slowed down. So wake up that metabolism and eat breakfast to start burning fat. **Remember to always consult your doctor when starting a new plan or diet.**

You Are

Beautiful

Your meals will be as follows:

First Plan

(see below for allowed proteins, starch carbs and fruits and portion sizes)

<u>Breakfast</u>

Protein

Starch Carbs

½ cup of fruit

<u>Snack</u>

Protein

½ cup of fruit

<u>Lunch</u>

Protein

Starch Carbs

Veggies

<u>Snack</u>

Protein

<u>Dinner</u>

Protein

Veggies

<u>Snack</u>

Protein

Proteins:

Roasted chicken breast, grilled chicken breast, roasted fish, grilled fish, lean turkey burger, turkey breast, tuna, egg whites, fat free cottage cheese (only this dairy is allowed now), protein shake, turkey sausages, salmon, or any other lean meats.

Protein Portion Sizes:

Chicken: 2 ½ ounces if you eat every three hours, or 4 ounces if you eat every four hours

Egg Whites: 4 extra-large eggs or 6 regular eggs

Protein Shake: 1 scoop

Cottage Cheese: 1 cup

Fish: 2 ½ ounces

Tuna: 1 can

Starch Carbs:

Grits, brown rice, oatmeal, yams, couscous, sweet potatoes.

Carbs Portion Sizes:

Grits: ½ cup

Brown Rice: 1 cup for lunch, ½ cup for dinner

Yams: ½ cup

<u>Veggies:</u>

Asparagus, broccoli, green beans, squash, eggplant, or any other veggie cooked whichever way you like except with no oils and definitely not fried. Corn, potatoes, peas, chickpeas, navy, pinto, refined, white and lima beans and squash are all considered starchy vegetables and should not be eaten to fulfill vegetable portions but to fulfill starch vegetable requirements. MayoClinic.com has a great list of acceptable non-starchy vegetables. You can also find recipes online for delicious meals.

<u>Veggies Portion Sizes:</u>
Always 1 cup

<u>Fruits:</u>

All fruits are allowed, but berries are especially good for you. You can add berries to your oatmeal in the morning or make a smoothie using berries and a little of your favorite natural fruit juice.

<u>Fruit Portion Sizes:</u>
Always ½ cup

Second Plan

You have to keep alternating eating plans so that your body does not settle and get used to one plan. When it does, your metabolism will become sluggish and your body will often begin storing fat instead of having it ready to be burned during exercise. In this next plan, you will alternate between day 1 and day 2.

Second Plan: Day 1 – Eat Every 4 Hours

Breakfast
Protein
Starch Carbs

Lunch
Protein
Veggies

Snack
Protein
Veggies

Dinner
Protein
Veggies

Second Plan: Day 2 – Eat Every 4 Hours

Breakfast

Protein

Lunch

Protein

Starch Carbs

Veggies

Snack

Protein

Veggies

Dinner

Protein

Starch Carbs

Veggies

If you feel you have reached a plateau and are not losing weight, mix it up a little and go back to the first plan and continue your exercise hobby.

The following supplements also help**, but always consult your doctor before taking any supplements:**

Liquid L-Carnitine: In the morning and before bed.

Omega-3 Fish Oil

Flax Seed Oil

CLA

Keep moving your body and stay away from processed foods, sugar, breads pasta and white rice. Once you get to your ideal weight you can incorporate these things once in a while; never every day because you will gain the weight back. Empower yourself and check out the things you put in your body. Read the label of the product you are eating and avoid the following: saturated and trans fats, high fructose corn syrup, Monosodium Glutamate (MSG), nitrite and sugar.

If you follow this plan, exercise, and you don't have any underlying medical conditions, most people will see results within one month! Enjoy!

Internet Safety

"The Internet is a giant international network of intelligent, informed computer enthusiasts, by which I mean, "people without lives." We don't care. We have each other...""

~ Dave Barry

The internet is a fun place full of information, games, funny videos and places to meet new people but it can also be extremely dangerous. Some sick people hide behind the mask of the internet. When you are in a chat room or answering an ad be VERY careful. The person you are talking to could be anyone. There have been criminal cases involving the internet like the Craigslist killer, a man who placed ads on Craigslist to meet women who he then robbed and killed. I had a friend that met a girl online and when he finally decided to meet her she was a man! There are stories about men and women who fell in love with someone they met online without meeting them in person only to be hurt and shocked when they realized the person they fell in love with was never real. Sadly, many individuals who are bored feel inadequate, or are living with a mental disease use the internet to lead a fantasy life. They pretend to be someone they are not and sometimes even the other sex! It is a fact that some people who decided to meet someone they had met online have been victims of theft and even murder. There's the story going around about a man that arranged to meet a girl in person that he had met online, but when he got into her car, there was another man in the back seat of the car asking for his money. He was brutally stabbed!

The internet is full of these stories if you look for them. On a funnier and kind of sick note, there are stories going around on the internet of a man who was dating a woman online for six months without exchanging pictures; the woman turned out to be his mother! I'm not kidding you. Look it up. You don't know who the person on the other side is. There have been incidents where a girl thought she was talking to a boy her age, but the boy was actually an older man. Sick people use these venues to lure young and unsuspecting victims either to rob, murder, rape, kidnap or even to enslave.

Therefore, when using the internet, consider what you have read here. Have fun, but always be careful. If you do decide to meet someone you have met online in person, take some precautions:

- Never give your real name or last name

- Do not upload pictures of yourself in chat rooms

- Never download anything without your parent's permission. Downloads can have hidden software to track you or find your location.

- Never ever share your passwords with anyone, except your parents

- Never meet a stranger alone

- Never meet a stranger at your house

- Never give your parents work schedule or parents routine to anyone online. They may use it to rob your home or worse!

- Never give a stranger the name of your school
- Never meet a stranger without telling your parents, even if you are going to meet in a group of friends.
- Don't let people online trick you into a fight
- Never give them your address or phone
- Never get into a stranger's car
- Never give them any personal details that they can use later to find you if you choose not to see them again.
- Meet new friends in a public place with lots of people.
- If after you meet them with a group of friends you decide that you want to continue getting to know this person, do so ALWAYS with a group of friends and in a public place where you will be safe.
- Always use your own car to go places and NEVER EVER get into someone's car that you and your parents don't know well.
- ALWAYS tell your parents or someone you can rely on where you are going to be and at what time you expect to come home in case anything happens to you. It is easier to follow a trail if the police know where to start looking. This can save your life!

- If someone is harassing or inappropriate with you online, tell your parents and report them to your internet service provider.

After going out for a long time, you can do a background investigation on the person. That way you will have a better idea of who they really are. And if they are hiding something from you, you will find out.

Use the internet for research, games and browsing, but be very careful if you use it to meet people. Consider yourself warned!

Sexting

"Any man who can drive safely while kissing a pretty girl is simply
not giving the kiss the attention it deserves."

~ Albert Einstein

A crush or a new love is so exciting and the feelings are so
powerful that it is common to feel you would do anything to get
or keep their attention.   Some people resort to sending sexy
pictures of themselves to their crush or sweetheart to keep them
interested. If you are considering doing this, you need to be aware
that sexting to a minor is illegal in some states (1) and other states
are expected to soon catch up and make it illegal under child
pornography laws.   Sending sexy pictures of yourself to a minor
can land you on the sexual offender's list. Even if you are a teen
and a minor yourself.   Not only you will get in trouble for
distributing child pornography, but the person receiving it can get
in legal trouble for possessing child pornography on their cell
phone as well. How happy do you think they will be with you
after you get them in trouble?

Sexting

There are lots of ways to get your crush to notice you, the right way. Read the chapter "Make Them Notice You." The advice in this chapter will show you how you can get your crush to notice you in a way that does not put you or him at a disadvantage if it does not work out between the two of you.

Teens that resort to sexting are placed in a vulnerable and dangerous position. Aside from being illegal, think about what will happen if you decide to break it off. Is he trustworthy enough not to brag about girls sending him naked pictures of themselves? What if he resents you for breaking up with him and decides to get back at you by sending your naked pictures to everybody in school. Remember how easy it is to share a photo on a cell phone. Anyone can also get a hold of his cell phone. What will happen if an ex-girlfriend, his mother, or one of his buddies browses through his cell phone pics? Your photo could be all over your school and the internet in a few minutes and his mother will not have a very high opinion of you. Worse yet, people may develop the wrong idea about you. This reputation will not be in your best interest when you finally meet your soul mate or when you're making new friends.

Let's say that you are older now and applying for your dream career that you've worked so hard for and the company does a background investigation, which is very common nowadays and quickly becoming the standard in the hiring process and your naked picture resurfaces on the internet. Do you think you will get the job? The answer is no, you won't.

What will happen when your new love decides to search for your name on the internet and your naked picture pops up? What do you think they are going to think of you? Once you post or send a picture of yourself you cannot take it back and there is always a chance that the picture will end up on the internet forever where anybody can see it such as parents, family members, friends, co-workers, your new boss or your new sweetheart, your children and your grandchildren. Your reputation will never be the same again and your new sweetheart and others may get the wrong idea of you.

The best thing to do when you get the urge to show your new crush how sexy you are is to restrain yourself and wait until your honeymoon. If your new love is pressuring you to send him a sexy photo of yourself remind him that this is illegal and it can cause lots of legal problems for him and you for the rest our your lives. Everlasting, true love is based on friendship, compatibility of personality types and trust. Your true love will love you for who you are, not your goods.

Sexting

$\mathcal{T}$een $\mathcal{S}afety$

"Danger never takes a holiday."

~ Unknown

As a teen, you have a bit more freedom and independence. You feel invincible and quite capable of taking care of yourself, but rest assured, that is not the case. The many unsolved missing teen cases will attest to this. It is very important that you always listen to your parents and follow the safety rules they teach you because as a new human, you don't yet have the life experience to know the dangers in the real world and how to prevent them. So read carefully and follow these rules to be safe:

- Always tell your parents, guardian, or a trusted adult where you are going to be and the phone number of the house where you will be. In case of an emergency, authorities will know where to start looking for you.
- Always let your parents know at what time you will be returning home. Sometimes when a person goes missing, time is of the essence and the faster they find you the

better chances you have to be found alive.

- Never give your address, phone number, school name, or any personal information to someone you just met; in other words a stranger.

- When you stay at a friend's house don't assume because you know your friend you also know their family. They could have a family member that is not safe for kids or adults. I would not recommend staying at a friend's house unless your parents know the family very well.

- Also, when staying at a friend's house, be aware if there are any home maintenance, phone repair, construction or any type workers in the house or nearby. If any of them are making you feel uncomfortable try to get away from them as quickly as possible. Leave or call your parents, let them know why you want to leave and ask them to pick you up. Is better to be home bored but safe.

- If anyone touches you in an inappropriate way, stop it immediately- scream and say, "NO!" Fight with all your strength. Put your fingers in their eyes, and if he is a man, hit or kick hard between their legs. Run to safety as fast as you can and tell someone what just happened. . Don't let that person intimidate you. They will try to discourage you from telling someone by threatening you or someone you love because they know they will be in trouble if you do tell. Don't be afraid, nothing bad will happen to you if you do tell. You did NOT do anything wrong. You did not deserve or cause this to happen in any way, even if you dressed provocatively. The person that tried being inappropriate with you is dangerous to other kids and possibly adults. He needs help or needs to be put away where he cannot hurt anyone again.

- Be aware of how you dress, certain sick individuals believe that girls that dress provocatively are looking for a sexual encounter with anyone, and teen boys do not really respect girls that dress too provocatively. Don't send the wrong message to sick individuals and dress more conservatively. Your soul mate will love you for you and not for how sexy you dress.

- If you are going out, always go in your own car. If something bad happens, you will have a way to quickly get out.

- Never, ever get in the car of someone you just met.

- Never, ever text while you are driving. Many teens have lost their lives this way. If you need to text, wait until you are somewhere safe.

- Never drive after you've had a drink. Even if you feel

fine to drive you are not. Alcohol interferes with the transmission of signals between the nerve cells in the muscles and the brain. Your reaction time to an emergency, such as a vehicle or a person getting in front of your car, will be slowed. Alcohol impairs your vision and judgment also. This is why many drunk drivers are found driving the wrong way on a street or highway.

- Never emotionally or physically hurt another person. Be kind. Everybody is dealing with their own problems and hurts, and you never know, you may be the one thing that drives that person over the top to commit suicide. There are too many suicides due to bullying. Don't contribute to the hate and pain in the world. Be kind; be a real life hero.

- Have a "safe word" between you and your parents or guardians. If your parents have an emergency and cannot contact you but send someone who knows your family's "safe word," you know that they were actually sent by your parents and are not a stranger. Never reveal this "safe word" to anyone.

- Similar to the rule above, have a "panic word" in case you are in trouble but cannot say it and somehow you are allowed to call or answer a phone call from your parents. They will know you are in trouble without you actually saying it.

- If you find yourself in trouble call 911. You don't have to speak directly to the operator just make sure the operator hears that you are in trouble. Don't hang up so that the authorities can trace the call back to your location and rescue you.

- Always carry your cell phone and when in trouble hide your phone and set it to silent. This way no one knows you still have a cell phone and you can still call 911.

- When an adult needs non-emergency help such as finding a dog or unloading something from their car, they can get help from other adults and should not approach kids or teenagers. If a stranger approaches you asking for your help, always keep your distance so that they cannot grab you. Apologize for not being able to help them and keep going.

- Never park your car next to a van at a busy parking lot such as a mall.

- Never use an ATM machine. Plan ahead and get money out of your account from inside a grocery store while purchasing something or from a bank. It is safer.

- When at the mall or similar parking lot, always leave the mall with your car keys in your hand and be aware of your surroundings. If you see a van parked next to your car go back to the store and ask a security guard to escort you to your car. If you feel someone is following you, go back to the store and ask a security guard to escort you.

- When you are home alone, do not answer your door and do not answer the house phone; let the answering machine answer. You do NOT want anyone knowing you are home alone.

- There are some people in this world who would try to gain the trust of kids by buying them presents, taking them where they want to go, and giving them what they want just to try to take advantage later. If you have such a person in your life and suddenly he starts to behave strangely; begins to touch you in an inappropriate way and makes you feel uncomfortable, stop hanging around him at once before anything bad happens. You do not owe him anything for the things he has given you. Tell your parents, guardian, or anyone what he said or how he treated you until someone listens, protects you and takes action to put him where he cannot hurt anyone ever again.

I hope this advice helps you as much as it helped me and the

Teen Life

kids I've known. Don't be hard on your parents or guardians and understand you are their treasure and they want the best for you: to be safe, healthy, and successful. Respect them, be smart and learn from them, they have already walked this path and have gone through what you are going through now. Be safe, be kind, be productive and enjoy your teen years!

The End

D. M. Mejias has a bachelor's degree in IT and business from FIU. She has lived in Florida and Missouri where she worked for the Missouri School District with kids of all ages and offered inspirational advice and guidance. She now lives in a small town in the hills of Missouri where she retreated to write her books.